FLIGHT OF AUGUST

FLIGHT OF AUGUST

Poems by Lawrence Eby

*Winner of the 2013 Louise Bogan Award
for Artistic Merit and Excellence*

Eby, Lawrence
1ˢᵗ edition.

ISBN: 978-0-9855292-5-3
Library of Congress Control Number: 2013945242

Interior Layout by Lea C. Deschenes
Cover Design by Dorinda Wegener
Cover Art by Darren Inouye
Editing by Terry Lucas

Printed in Tennessee, USA
Trio House Press, Inc.
Fernandina Beach, FL
Ponte Vedra Beach, FL

To contact the author, send an email to submissions@triohousepress.org

For my father...

FLIGHT OF AUGUST

I.

We scout.

The pelt line is empty
   swaying hard to the ever-winter
   wind. The cold cold
nails jutting from collapsed
shanties, sheets hung
from a rebar post

   cinderblocks circle the tent
   to guard what we have:

water jugs
twelve bullets
a mandolin.

Out of some paint-peeled door, there is a white flag
slapping at the air.

2.

Meander the bucket over, pour
        the fire out, our
        smokeless need to stealth
        in desert, our smoke-

    filled bodies. The body is,
    it is asking, a pass between
    the bushes, a hideaway

in an attic. What happens when
        you become a refugee
        to the earth itself? These
        bundled things walking

    for friction, there's a destination
    over the next mountain
    pass. Freeways kneel

and hold their arms out for
        collapse for collapse.

3.

Banquet halls with place-settings
still ripe, the white
      tablecloths with a coat of old

In here, son.
In here.
        There's a cupboard of cans.

Don't fidget with the napkins.

      The boy polishes and pockets
      a fork, a spoon, the white cloth
      napkin in his shirt pocket now.

Hail beats the roof, heavy wind
tweaks the walls and for once
there's no rush to keep
moving.

Eat.

4.

Billowing endless
        clouds   smoke   dried up forest burning,
        burning
the last hovels from the branch-elbows.

                magazine
                pen
                dressings

        in the ignited sedan, a body down the path
        with a broken leg. There are ghosts

somewhere inside these mounds of leaves. A cabin
is not vacant. Occupied with the still and settled
dust. Jiggle the knob crank the

        door. A candle burns atop the stove a
fleshy smell. There's someone here breathing-
                                in the rest of the air.

5.

I stand in the doorway and watch
this man drive by. He cannot

see me in the crevices of this city and hasn't
for these long cold days.

There is something about his
search that feels at home. He

goes from house to house
and pulls things from wreckage:

> cans of fruit
> blankets
> a dog collar.

Outside the city, he
keeps these trinkets in a pile,

his tent sways in the gale. He sorts through,
pausing at each forest sound.

6.

The first February snow

      light
              on the eaves, our

sliding glass   door
needs   sealant
      beneath the boarded up
the empty propane tank in the back
yard   o-rings dryworn rot and we've buried

those needing to be buried, we've

scavenged toward Spring.
Stay up in shifts, all waking   to any lights
round the cul-
       de-sac. This space is ours

as long as we don't lose footing,   if we don't
lose to this frozen sea.

7.

Reach for the sickle
      hide the wine. It won't be long
before bandits arrive.   Shutters on windows,
the rattling, rattling
stampedes of ice down
        wooden peaks. the city's on fire; cornfield frozen

a dryness in your throat. What occurs
      when sun hides in hail? A mouse crawls
      across rafter beams, catch it, catch it

before it vanishes to the snow-filled *out.*

8.

        Bottles lined

up

    on the picket

fence.

       Take aim, son.
       Take aim, son.
       This is what survival becomes.

    hammer
       clicks   snapped
            gunfire
       shat   ters   bir
       ds   from   the   trees
       gla   ss   from   the
            fence.

There will be

    meals on the spit

the skinny

    meat   starved

itself

    at least it's something.

9.

This cabin has been in the family for
   four generations and now I hide beneath
floorboards hold my breath and

there: creaking across the living room
        these strangers
clear the stove,

rummage through drawers,
       take
what they need. I've become

reclusive in the ever-winter. I hold
the air inside me. A widow's

nest crawling around my head. I'm dying
for contact. Some human touch
warmth among the frost-burst pipes.   Do I

speak?

10.

Go to the well and draw
    the bucket we're
in need don't   We
you see?   Just don't
        have much left
    running low on that
last bag of grain.

II.

He kicks in the door.
He opens the cabinets
to the dust
      empty, the empty
      cavity bubbling inside,

      he moves on. Pines shake at the wind, gray blanket sky
freckled with sparrows searching soil for worm, seed atop a
frozen grave. Their eggs are solid in the nest, unable to crack.

      Beaks freeze-pressed
      against the egg wall.

We are stuck in the dome
                is there escape?
He runs, runs
until the cliffside bowl feels like a terrible womb.

12.

There's a camp in the woods
where the breathers gather. Their chests
pulse together fueling the fire
dead heaped and wrapped. They eat

from a fresh harvest of asparagus
spend the night breeding
in sleeping bags, tents with tears in the flap. These pleasures

locked in the town-fire, the plunder
of those who strip brass from pipes. The cold creeps

     in, sucks

life from inside
them. A boy scrapes a maple
     with his knife to the frozen
syrup underneath.

13.

Why won't the snow end?

14.

       chip
       the
       granite
nose of a man smelling the end. Ground
littered with pieces of himself shaped like wilted lotus.

       So much smashed glass
       in the financial district,
a chatter, a chatter in rafters, two children prying open
       a can of peaches. Hush, hush yourselves, the engine
roars
       searchlight for bounty.

15.

Fire escape shakes stripped screws
      we descend to a parked taxi,
      roof rusted peeling paint,
          windshield shattered, we step from
          stairs to hood. Creaks
to feet. The snowy ground puffs out in clouds
      as we venture to the next open door,
the next unscavenged cabinets.

16.

Cotton-candy seven days old in a coat pocket,
                    waves overcome with severed limbs
          step wooden plank the knocking,
the knocking, seagulls suck worms from the bottle,
        skylight orange, fisherman's bucket

knocked to the sand. Zip-tied telephone lines: a trap
        to lure a bird/meal. The ocean's

        travelers   dock to pillage,
dock to fetch quench beacon old buildings.
                 a seagull, a man
                       hiding under the floor boards,
            watching, a rat trapped by his feet
                      still breathing.

17.

These gray branches with bulbs of rotted oranges
scattered on the tundra.

> There's something about how these trees move,
> wind gusting the frozen spurs
> their creaking before the crack.

> You can almost hear them moan
> across the barren undergrowth,
> the seeds with ears

> closed, bodies exposed to the non-living,
> prey to anything with working
> hands. Flip venison in the skillet,

> huddle on the groundsheet,

keep the lights
> *dim,*

boy. It's rare to bloom out here.

18.

Fireflies spark through the chains
        a rusted swing-set, rubber seat black wet.
        a fresh tire rolls in the torrent
gutter.
                Driver wire-eyed
                peers in the windows at
                movement, drapes writhe

                closed, breaks

ease squeak, and the door
        is open. stag living

        behind the curtain. It scratches

at the cloth, claws
of winter biting the driver's
hair.

19.

I hear there is a wheat field up north.

Uh-huh. Growing in the ice?

They said the sun comes out up there.

Who's they?

Just overheard it. Whispers in the camp.

Don't trust nothin' you hear. No
such thing as good news.

20.

The oaks white and flowing,
    a hand buried with fingers

out in the cold, it reaches
    like the city's buildings, peaking

peaking out whitegray, a fire
    pulses toward steel, the wood, glass

    is broken, a family of four survives
the night and maybe the morning,

the month grim and tethered to
    the ever-winter, these fingers,

    buildings reaching toward the same
pinnacle, the outside shell
    of this spinning marble.

21.

A desk melts into the tile floor, the windows
cracked and browning. A forest of homes

        caught fire to dry cold,
        lightning struck
        Joshua tree,

                build the fire, son
                build the fire, son
                chilled wind is a devil's claw.

        No one is clean among
        burning pines, ashen snow mixed in the bottle
earth
is.   Crows nest atop
        streetlamps, cawing

                at the last frozen hand stuck
                to the curb's edge.

        No is loud out here. Echoing
        off windows,
an echo

breaks icicles from the eaves.
A fire in the distance
counts victims.

22.

Forest beyond burns and inside an abandoned house: a survivor watches the glow on the wall, the crawling of it, the too much cold. Shoes with holes, wrestling wind, pageant trophies knocked off the shelf. The power is out, and he's low on living. The telephone is ringing with no one on the line, and he watches his shadow grow and shrink into the cycles of night, and almost night. The door is nailed shut, chimney plugged—the winter is hissing its way across the window's sill.

23.

We fled to the desert in search
of heat.
      We lost three the first
night, nine of us left. We just

didn't know night's cold, we didn't
anticipate shrubs sucking up
our only water.

24.

For a brief moment
                     the sun blazes electromagnetic

stop signs ignite a reflection, this light
        pulsing & melting the ice road,   a woman birthed
         a daughter
        and shows her this old past life. She holds the warmth
        to her cheeks. It is now

that these buildings feel alive. They jitter to boiling sounds,
                                the hot enough to fight
against this cold, this ever-winter
        pushed back like a ship displaces water.

          Hold up your hands, grab as much
          as you can.
        The opening is short and we've
        already felt the water collapse the hull.

25.

The stag breeds when the streetlamps flicker off.

26.

We found a desert hovel

           no doors or windows
           just openings, little dry wounds
           in the homely—the roof's palms
           with holes to the Milky Way's
           stars this lack of light is our only

our only. The comfort of a roof,
walls to block out the wind.

    We'll survive the night.
    In the morning we'll seek

    full our stomachs. There must be, must be
something growing in the ever-winter sea.

27.

Radio static, the antenna snapped
and hanging,
     the taste of sulfur tallying the air.
Leaves tombstoned on the carpet. A crow flies
through the open door to hunt.
     Mice hide in the walls, and one
     is stuck in the bathtub,
      clawing at the slick fiberglass cage.

28.

There's a body in the telephone booth and you don't
                even glance, you
     don't even take a moment
to see if it breathes.

          I've grown to love you.

But it's tiresome to trail behind.
     These fences cut my hands each
time I climb
       to avoid the street,
       to avoid your view.

          I've grown to love you.

But living exposed and unexposed,
the snow in and out of my socks,
       fire closing in on the dry city.

       I've grown to love you,
       but I have to let you go.

So, go. Please. Go.

29.

In this house we built dreaming
the heater breathes hot an August

day, the hearth grows blackberries
instead of fire   and we   now

       see all our dead on
       the lawn, living and gathered for harvest

       a meal warm, soft, and ripe
       French toast, molasses, a baked hen

       the seeds of the lively
       planted. growing.   but the veil

       is gone and the cold
       stalks us from behind the trees.

       the stag   horned-
       devil   tracks our

       need to live and die.
       It sleeps in a liminal

       cavern, both inside
       and outside of the burning tundra.

30.

South town   these streets
slink the river mud from a barrel of trees outgrowing

their pots. These roots cut
through a telephone pole sleeping on a house
where a new tribe builds

effigies made of carburetors. They lay
naked in the snow.
                Not much has changed.
                Just numbers.

One chair left at a square table.

31.

When you glance at the watch
in the shift minute a coyote

reaches between the bushes growing
in an alleyway, a candle burns

upstairs in a near-empty tire factory. You're
tired of walking—I can

see it in your feet, the way
they drag through the slosh. I've been

watching you these past
three weeks. The crows

have been living cleaner lives, and unlike
you, kill only to survive.

> You'll get yours when the pigeons
> nest in your hair.

32.

Around the desert
campfire we tell
stories of *things*
hidden in the caves,
hanging in the forest's
trees. There are
ephemeral claws
in the old bank
skyscrapers, each
floor its own
lair. And those
who dare enter
have never
returned. We know
these stories
as truth. We all
know someone
lost in the white
halls, some vanish
in the pile-
d leaves. Keep
your feet
tucked when you
sleep. The frost
is another devil
to fear.

33.

When the smoke plumes
     grow fainter
When the sea
     grows bluer

where is the vanish,
where is the tide?

These human constructs have swollen like a grapefruit in a fire.

Will a gate be a gate when language is gone?
     Will we all just end up as fragments in the air,
attracted to the atmospheric edge, a blanket of singularities
pulling at our threads?
     This shelled–off earth, a dew drop on the cosmic leaf.

34.

Horseman in the alley, tight rein bounty from the night
before, blood on his boots, this asphalt clicking,
clicking jaw when he opens
wide, yells
stop.
Woman, hair
tight-bound slick, she behind
a thin door locked, him and his crew knocking,
knocking it unhinged. Them hunched in a pile, her gunshot
voice. She alive behind a table, breathing.

35.

A library hideout, generator chugs away

in the reading room, the cables

shaped as the wall's crack. In the office, we lean

back in the swivel chairs, a television glows

Twilight Zone, the old gray pixels

bring us way, way when there was

more color, less silt,

living bodies filling these library chairs.

36.

Sleet through the dry oaks
an ant-filled robin rots on a sheet
roof. The

ground is littered with
them, these
dead birds,

their bodies in various
decay. Lack of food, trees

dormant in the ever-winter.
A bundled man left
atop a pile of

leaves, frozen soil:
the unbreakable grave.

37.

With pliers she pinches at the back of her
  ankle, it's so gray
  outside, and the only thing left
  is to remove the finger-sized splinter
sticking out her
skin. The torn animal, the season
shifting out the ground. When
it doesn't let the roof collapse,
  the river in the street
  is undrinkable. Where is the pharma-
  cist? When are we ready to die.

38.

grind coffee
        cull the playground
scavenge school
        rain dance
weave blanket
        gather wood
build fire
        put fire out
dig
        dig
collect worms
        fish
hide
        cold burns
your
        lips
tight

39.

August leaves its dry
heat-floats across the arid
plain.

      This is the last time.

Burnt calendars at city hall, people
bundled in their parkas. This is before

      they've seen all the building's crumbs
      trailing to an empty well.

This is before the woodstack dwindles.

40.

It's been a week since I let you go. The last
pack of coyotes has dwindled

to three.   And now, I
am injured, the buildings sway

to this bludgeoning wind. I miss
            watching you. Our first

day   me behind
the fence   you driving

looking for something.
The windows sulk

in the crystallized frost,
the dirty glass, brown chilled

broken.

41.

The clothesline garments

        sunfaded wilt,
        grayed with ash. A bucket
        below them filled

with snow, the ice
at the bottom
solid. A wooden door

is cracked, a hole
in the rail splinter-jagged
an opening for

        wild-
        life scuttling
across the sills,

        the glass droops,
        quiet ambiance
cresting the slate roof.

The boy and his father push through
the door and feel the hanging threads.

        They're stiff with cold
        and this warmth will do.

42.

Clock shop smashed in the riot
the riot. Two burning

cars in the street, melted
      dash, the pedals pinned

to the floor. There's no gas
      left in

         the   station
         's   bathroom

         locked shut

     water running down
     the drain   the aisles

emptied of their goods.
      A stag in the street

in the crosshairs.

43.

When thinking of flight, the body emerges a wing. Its feathers transparent against the blue-gray, those subtle tones   roof tones   wall tones   a checkered floor with a layer of dust, a hand-trail cleared black and white squares with a corner tugged up. The underneath on the cusp

of bloom. How many people have traveled through this kitchen? The thin cabinet doors open, bare shelves. On the counter, the telephone is off the hook. Unpaid bills, a calendar marked

in X's. A stencil of a wasp on the kitchen table is bedded with dust. The desperate animal abandons its nest, flees gliding to the tundra's deep burn.

44.

The boy and his father approach.
         It is caught in a car window, antlers

tearing at the seats.   The windshield
         is cracked, the animal
         is bleeding from its neck.

         Do not approach
         it, wait for the calm.

It twists its body, pulls. Clatter of hooves
         on asphalt. Grunts,
      seethes, the boy approaches, and his
         father carries a bough.
Stay back.   A swing, a clack, the temple cut
         and loose the blood. The stag limps a steady
        breath.   The father wrestles
         the head from the window, shredded
   fabric roof   his feet   sliding icy road. He leaves
         the animal lay in the street
to wake alive in falling snow.

45.

Movement is the only
illusion. Particle dust

gleams in the attic, movements
of the unreal, movements where

an animal steps into the tundra
for a breath of fresh smoke. The earth is tired

of its rotation. The sun
is sore from long years

of weight. These globed children and their
demands. The grandchildren are asking for water,

clean water. We are the grandchildren. There is
no inheritance in the envelope. We

spent the copper, spent
the nickel. We are

beyond a repairman's callused
work, his touch. Just keep moving, keep

the all in its place
for a while longer. A beast

unsettles its own cave,
we hear the rumble.

46.

The stag's horns reach up the hillside;
saplings sprouting against the mire.

47.

The boy wakes to his father gone. He wakes to the sound of a cat's meow. He wakes to the gray city in its snow of ash. The boy wakes and feels alone. His waking is what startles him the most. He wakes and stands and searches. He wakes the dust behind him. He wakes to his fear of being alone. The boy wakes and looks across the city for movement, a sign of his father. He wakes and checks what is left of the fresh water. He wakes to worry. He wakes to wonder. He wakes to a world in which he no longer belongs. He wakes to his father on the second-story balcony, binoculars rested on his cheeks, scouting. He wakes to what this is and what it will become.

48.

August returns to siphon the fires, to
     restore itself on the calendar,
                mice drink from an oasis,
                palms scraping at the sky,

     return, return. The turning of the globe
   a necessity to nothing, just the burdens of matter's
hunger for matter's hunger. All these

tarpaulin camps   houses without windows   stoneless
   graves
         return, return. Let the world spin,

  let the body be, let this vine crown
       the curve of a steel bridge's wires; ride

the wake to the collision of birth, return, return. A blue jay
        sings to its eggs, to their future of hatch
              and flight.

Acknowledgments

Thank you to the following journals in which these poems have appeared, sometimes under different numbers: *THRUSH Poetry Journal,* "3" and "6"; *The Pacific Review,* "1"; **Cleaver Magazine,** "4", "12" and "21"; *Dead Flowers: A Poetry Rag,* "7" and "16"; *Berkley Poetry Review,* "39", "42" and "43".

I would also like to thank my mentors at California State University—San Bernardino, Chad Sweeney, Julie Sophia Paegle, and Juan Delgado, for all of their insights into making this manuscript come alive. And a huge thanks to my cohort and the cohort that came before: Ashley Hayes, André Katkov, Natalie Skeith, s.Nicholas, Casey Goodson, Kelly Dortch, Meghan McCarthy, Isaac Escalera, and Tristan Acker.

Thank you to my PoetrIE family whose feedback and support during this project was tremendous: Cindy Rinne, Jason E. Keller, Isabel Quintero-Flores, Ryan Mattern, Aaron Reeder, Michael "Mouse" Cooper, Cherie Rouse, and all those who dropped in from time to time.

Thank you to my family for being open about my pursuit in the arts, and supporting me along this crazy journey.

Thank you to Joan Houlihan for believing in these poems. And last but not least, a huge thank you to everyone at Trio House Press who worked tirelessly to make this book into what it is today.

About the Author

Lawrence Eby writes from Southern California and is currently finishing his MFA at California State University – San Bernardino. He volunteers time on the Inlandia Institute's Publications Committee, is a founding member of PoetrIE, an Inland Empire-based literary community and is Founder and Editor-in-Chief of Orange Monkey Publishing, a small poetry press. At CSUSB, he spent time as the Poetry Editor for *Ghost Town*, the school's national literary magazine.

About the Artist

Darren Inouye is a young, up and coming artist with a passion to create compelling imagery mixing the themes of faith, spirituality, and the journey of man on this earth through mixed media. His images use stark graphic shapes mixed with organic painterly strokes to great powerful images. Having studied Illustration at the Pasadena Art Center College of Design, Darren desires to create narratives through his work that can impact culture and the direction of the creative arts for a more positive tomorrow. Check out his work at www.darrenin.com.

About the Book

Flight of August was designed at Trio House Press
through the collaboration of:

Terry Lucas, Lead Editor
Darren Inouye, Cover Art: *Above the Storms*
Dorinda Wegener, Cover Design
Lea Deschenes, Interior Design

The text is set in Adobe Caslon Pro.

The publication of this book is made possible, whole or in part,
by the generous support of the following individuals and/or agencies:

Anonymous

About the Press

Trio House Press is a collective press. Individuals within our organization come together and are motivated by the primary shared goal of publishing distinct American voices in poetry. All THP published poets must agree to serve as Collective Members of the Trio House Press for twenty-four months after publication in order to assist with the press and bring more Trio books into print. Award winners and published poets must serve on one of four committees: Production and Design, Distribution and Sales, Educational Development, or Fundraising and Marketing. Our Collective Members reside in cities from New York to San Francisco.

Trio House Press adheres to and supports all ethical standards and guidelines outlined by the CLMP.

The Editors of Trio House Press would like to thank Joan Houlihan.

Trio House Press, Inc. is dedicated to the promotion of poetry as literary art, which enhances the human experience and its culture. We contribute in an innovative and distinct way to American Poetry by publishing emerging and established poets, providing educational materials, and fostering the artistic process of writing poetry. For further information, or to consider making a donation to Trio House Press, please visit us online at: www.triohousepress.org.

Other Trio House Press Books you might enjoy:

The Consolations by John W. Evans
      2013 Trio Award Winner selected by Mihaela Moscaliuc

The Ghosts of Lost Animals by Michelle Bonczeck Evory, 2013

Fellow Odd Fellow by Steven Riel, 2013

Clay by David Groff
      2012 Louse Bogan Winner selected by Michael Waters

Gold Passage by Iris Jamahl Dunkle
      2012 Trio Award Winner selected by Ross Gay

If You're Lucky Is a Theory of Mine by Matt Mauch, 2012

CPSIA information can be obtained at www.ICGtesting.com
Printed in the USA
LVOW06s0515070114

368405LV00002B/6/P